WHATEVER HAPPENED TO...

THE SHANG DYNASTY?

BY KIRSTY HOLMES

BookLife PUBLISHING

©2019
BookLife Publishing Ltd.
King's Lynn
Norfolk, PE30 4LS

All rights reserved.
Printed in Malaysia.

A catalogue record for this book is available from the British Library.

ISBN: 978-1-78637-886-6

Written by:
Kirsty Holmes

Edited by:
John Wood

Designed by:
Dan Scase

All facts, statistics, web addresses and URLs in this book were verified as valid and accurate at time of writing.

No responsibility for any changes to external websites or references can be accepted by either the author or publisher.

BC AND AD

In this book, you will see **BC** after and **AD** before some dates. And some of the dates might look backwards. What's going on?

AD stands for Anno Domini and that means 'in the year of the Lord'. Christian calendars count forwards from the year that Christians believe Jesus Christ was born. When you see AD, you are counting forwards on the timeline.
AD 1750 = 1750 years after Jesus was born.

BC stands for Before Christ. If you see this next to a date, it means this happened before the birth of Jesus Christ. When you see BC, you are counting backwards on the timeline.
1750 BC = 1750 years before Jesus was born.

When describing a range of dates, you always count forwards.
So "between 1500 and 500 BC" or "from AD 500 to AD 1500" is correct.

Check back here if you need to.

2000 BC   1500 BC   1000 BC   500 BC   JESUS

WRITE THE YEAR AND THEN BC

CONTENTS

PAGE 4   WHATEVER HAPPENED TO THE SHANG DYNASTY?
PAGE 6   WHAT WAS THE SHANG DYNASTY?
PAGE 8   THE FALL OF THE XIA
PAGE 10   A DYNASTY IS BORN
PAGE 12   WRITTEN IN THE STARS
PAGE 14   THE GOOD EMPERORS
PAGE 16   DI XIN
PAGE 18   DA JI
PAGE 20   THE PLANETS ALIGN
PAGE 22   THE BATTLE OF MUYE
PAGE 24   INTO THE FIRE
PAGE 26   RISE AND FALL
PAGE 28   WHAT REMAINS OF THE ANCIENTS?
PAGE 30   GLOSSARY
PAGE 32   INDEX

WORDS THAT LOOK LIKE THIS ARE EXPLAINED IN THE GLOSSARY ON PAGES 30 AND 31.

BORN

AD 500   AD 1000   AD 1500   AD 2000

WRITE AD AND THEN THE YEAR

WHATEVER HAPPENED TO THE SHANG DYNASTY?

Imagine ancient China. Are you picturing lots of noble warriors in shining armour? Maybe you're imagining **SCRIBES** creating beautiful picture-writing? But if you went to China today, you wouldn't read your fortune on **ORACLE BONES**, or stroll around the city of Yin Xu admiring the bronze and pottery for sale at the market. But why is that? Where did the **CULTURE**, people and traditions of one of the world's oldest and most **ICONIC CIVILISATIONS** go?

IT'S THE LATEST FASHION!

THIS IS A DRAGON-SHAPED GONG FROM THE SHANG DYNASTY. IT IS MADE OF BRONZE.

OUT WITH THE OLD AND IN WITH THE NEW

It's easy to forget that ancient peoples were just like us in many ways. They had families, jobs, homes and leaders, just like we do. But life as they knew it then was very different to life as we know it now. Modern China is a wonderful mix of ancient traditions and modern technology. What would the ancient Shang people have thought about our modern world? In this book, we will take a look at how the **DYNASTY** of the Shang **EMPERORS** ended, and what they left behind...

THIS IS THE TOMB OF FU HAO, A FAMOUS SHANG QUEEN, FOUND IN THE CITY OF YIN XU. YOU CAN VISIT THIS ANCIENT CITY TODAY.

WAIT, WHAT?
TO PRONOUNCE THESE WORDS, SAY:
YIN XU = YIN SHU
FU HAO = FOO HOW

TURN ➔ THE PAGES OF HISTORY!

5

WHAT WAS THE SHANG DYNASTY?

WHERE ON EARTH?

The Shang dynasty lasted from 1600 to 1046 BC and was in eastern China (as we would know it today). The purple parts of this map show the areas that the Shang dynasty controlled, and the red dots show the many **CAPITAL CITIES** they used over time.

SHANG CIVILISATION

• Shang capitals

Drawn by Yu Ninjie

FAMOUS FOR BEING:
- Writers
- Craftspeople
- Farmers
- Bronze workers

THESE WEAPONS ARE MADE FROM BRONZE, WHICH IS A TYPE OF METAL. THE SHANG WERE MASTERS AT WORKING WITH BRONZE.

THE MANDATE OF HEAVEN

Emperors in Shang times believed that the gods had given them the right to rule. An important part of this was to remember to keep up their part of the deal – the gods would let them rule, but they had to use this power for the good of the people. If they did not, the gods would send a sign to say that person had lost the right to rule. Later dynasties, such as the Zhou, would call this the Mandate of Heaven, but the idea is as old as the Shang, and maybe even older...

> I AM SHANGDI, AN ANCIENT GOD IN CHARGE OF CHOOSING EMPERORS. I HAVE MANY NAMES. SOME CALL ME THE JADE EMPEROR. SOME CALL ME YUDI. BUT YOU CAN CALL ME MR HEAVEN. I HAVE TO KEEP AN EYE ON THOSE PESKY MORTALS - SOME EMPERORS CAN GET A BIT POWER-CRAZY. BUT IF THEY DO, I WILL LET THEM KNOW, AND A NEW EMPEROR WILL BE CHOSEN. SO WATCH OUT, SHANG DYNASTY! I'VE GOT MY EYE ON YOU.

SOCIAL SUCCESS

The people of the Shang dynasty were divided into different **SOCIAL CLASSES**. At the top was the royal family. Below the royal family came the ruling classes, made up of rich, important people with a lot of power. Below them were the priests, warriors, craftsmen, traders and farmers. Slaves were at the very bottom of the order of importance. Most people in Shang times were farmers.

> I'M A FARMER... ALL MY FRIENDS ARE FARMERS... MY CHILDREN ARE FARMERS... ALL THE BEST PEOPLE ARE, YOU KNOW.

WAIT, WHAT?
TO PRONOUNCE THESE WORDS, SAY:

SHANGDI = SHANG-DEE
ZHOU = JOE

7

THE FALL OF THE XIA

Most of this book will look at the end of the Shang dynasty. However, to understand the end you need to know how it started. Let's go back a very, very long way...

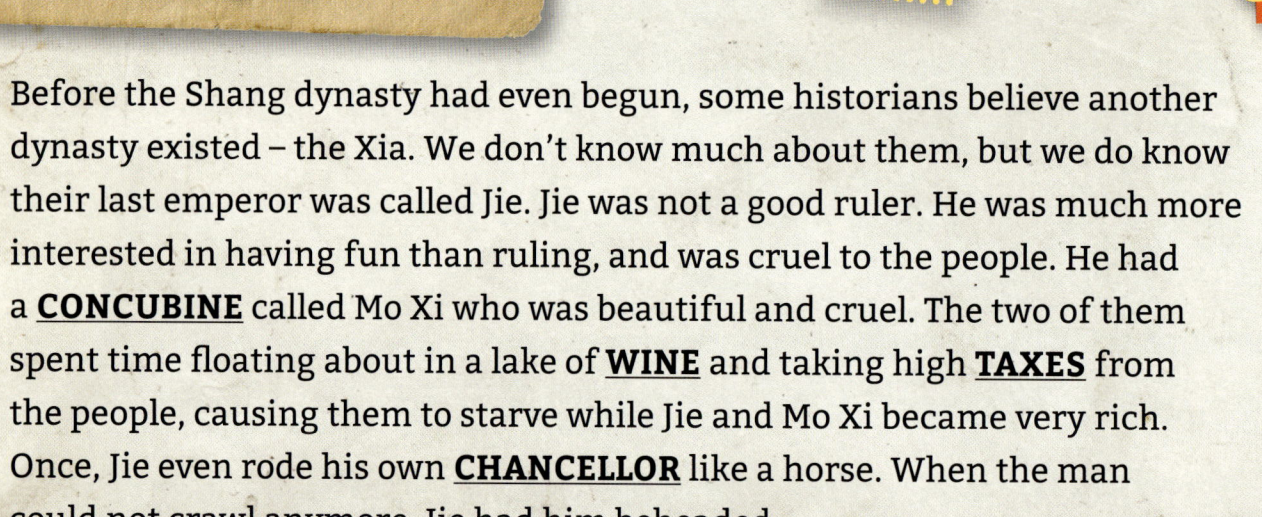

Before the Shang dynasty had even begun, some historians believe another dynasty existed – the Xia. We don't know much about them, but we do know their last emperor was called Jie. Jie was not a good ruler. He was much more interested in having fun than ruling, and was cruel to the people. He had a **CONCUBINE** called Mo Xi who was beautiful and cruel. The two of them spent time floating about in a lake of **WINE** and taking high **TAXES** from the people, causing them to starve while Jie and Mo Xi became very rich. Once, Jie even rode his own **CHANCELLOR** like a horse. When the man could not crawl anymore, Jie had him beheaded.

A man called Tang ruled the kingdom of Shang, which was a **STATE** under the rule of the Xia. He saw that Jie had become mad with power. Tang knew he had to get rid of Jie...

> HMM. THIS JIE SEEMS LIKE A BAD GUY. SOMEONE SHOULD DO SOMETHING...

THE AREA THOUGHT TO BE RULED BY THE XIA DYNASTY

WAIT, WHAT?
TO PRONOUNCE THESE WORDS, SAY:
XIA = SHAH
MO XI = MO SHEE

9

A DYNASTY IS BORN

TANG

Tang saw how the Emperor Jie of the Xia dynasty had become evil, and how he had forgotten to look after the people. Tang led the people in a **REVOLT**, defeating Jie at the Battle of Mingtiao. During a huge thunderstorm, Tang took the throne from Jie. The Shang dynasty had begun.

*THAT LAST EMPEROR WAS SO SILLY AND WAY TOO RICH. I WILL BE A GOOD EMPEROR, AND SET A GOOD EXAMPLE FOR ALL THOSE WHO FOLLOW ME. I'LL MAKE TAXES LOWER, LOOK AFTER THE POOR AND TAKE CARE OF MY PEOPLE. WE WILL HAVE PEACE AND **PROSPERITY**. WE WON THE BATTLE, SO IT IS CLEAR THE GODS ARE ON OUR SIDE. I THINK I'LL START A DYNASTY...*

ONE OF THE GOOD GUYS

Tang was known for being a good ruler — he even offered himself as a **SACRIFICE** to the gods when a **DROUGHT** threatened the people. Thankfully it rained just in time and he was saved — phew! He set a good example for the emperors that followed him, and for a long time the Shang emperors looked after the people well.

I am a high officer of the court of Tai Wu, the ninth emperor of the Shang Dynasty. Last week, we found mulberry trees growing right in the middle of the court. I told the king that the gods must have done it because he isn't ruling very well and is too interested in parties. Sure enough, he's promised to start behaving, and now the trees are withering away.

MULBERRY TREE

WRITTEN IN THE STARS

The ancient people of the Shang took the gods very seriously. People (especially the emperors) looked for signs that they were doing a good job. They believed the gods had many ways of showing the people how they felt, and signs and **DIVINATION** were very important. **ORACLES** and fortune tellers would advise the emperor, and important decisions would be taken based on their findings.

... WILL WE WIN THE BATTLE?

... SHOULD I INVADE THE NEXT KINGDOM?

... WILL OUR BABY BE A SON?

... WHAT SHALL WE HAVE FOR TEA?

ORACLE BONES

Ancient emperors used oracle bones to talk to the gods. These were usually ox bones or tortoise shells. The oracle (sometimes one of the emperor's wives) would write or scratch questions for the gods onto the bones, then burn them. The bones would crack in the fire, and the oracle would read the pattern of cracks as a message from the gods.

CAN YOU SEE THE WRITING ON THIS ANCIENT ORACLE BONE? WHAT QUESTIONS WOULD YOU ASK THE GODS?

How did a dynasty with such a strong connection to the gods disappear? We're going to look at how it all went horribly wrong. It's a great story. Let's go and find out — whatever happened to the Shang dynasty?

THE GOOD EMPERORS

A TIME OF GROWTH

During the first half of the Shang dynasty, the rulers were mostly good and the **EMPIRE** did well. Because the soil on the banks of the Yellow River was so **FERTILE**, the Shang people could easily grow enough food for themselves. This meant they could spend time on other things. The Shang people were able to invent a lot of new stuff, and get really good at working with bronze.

THE YELLOW RIVER IS THE SECOND-LONGEST RIVER IN CHINA. THE FIRST ANCIENT CHINESE CIVILISATIONS STARTED ALONG THE RIVER.

STICK THEM WITH THE POINTY END

The Shang were especially good at making weapons from bronze. They developed new weapons such as spears, knives, bows and arrows, and they also made tough armour. At the time, these were very deadly weapons, and the Shang were pretty hard to beat. The empire was always at war with barbarians and other empires who wanted to take over.

WU DING

Emperor **Wu Ding**'s <u>REIGN</u> was the longest of all the Shang emperors. One of his <u>CONSORTS</u>, Fu Hao, was a great military general herself, and may even have commanded an army of over 13,000 men. Many people think Wu Ding might have been the best emperor of the Shang dynasty.

THIS IS A DAGGER-AXE, CALLED A GE.

I AM FU HAO, CONSORT TO WU DING. I'M NOT LIKE SOME OF THE OTHER CONSORTS, WHO LIKE TO MESS ABOUT WITH ORACLE BONES ALL DAY OR GET DRESSED UP. NOT ME. CHECK OUT MY AXE. I MEAN BUSINESS.

DI XIN

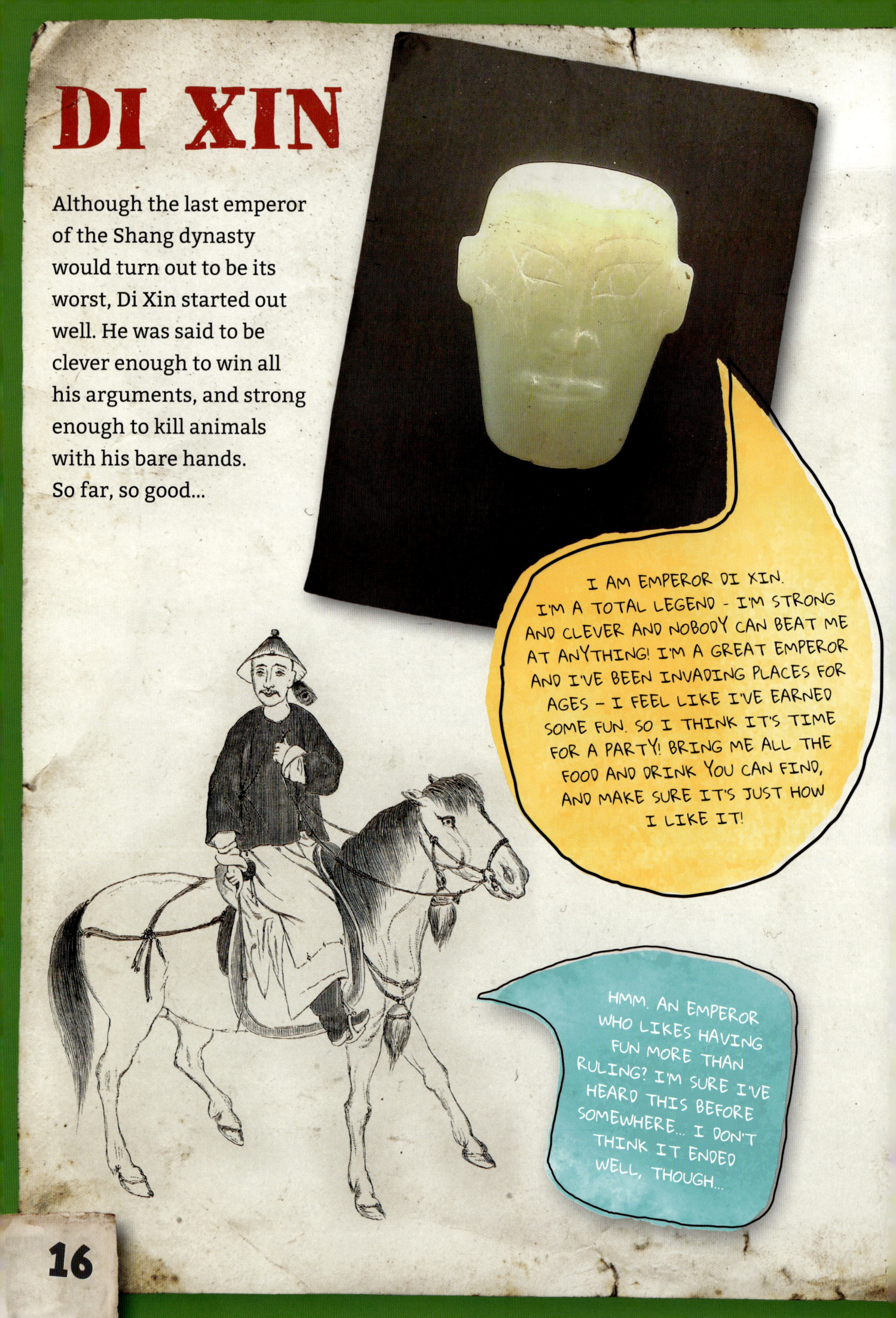

Although the last emperor of the Shang dynasty would turn out to be its worst, Di Xin started out well. He was said to be clever enough to win all his arguments, and strong enough to kill animals with his bare hands. So far, so good...

> I AM EMPEROR DI XIN. I'M A TOTAL LEGEND - I'M STRONG AND CLEVER AND NOBODY CAN BEAT ME AT ANYTHING! I'M A GREAT EMPEROR AND I'VE BEEN INVADING PLACES FOR AGES - I FEEL LIKE I'VE EARNED SOME FUN. SO I THINK IT'S TIME FOR A PARTY! BRING ME ALL THE FOOD AND DRINK YOU CAN FIND, AND MAKE SURE IT'S JUST HOW I LIKE IT!

> HMM. AN EMPEROR WHO LIKES HAVING FUN MORE THAN RULING? I'M SURE I'VE HEARD THIS BEFORE SOMEWHERE... I DON'T THINK IT ENDED WELL, THOUGH...

Di Xin decided to invade and conquer the small state of the Lord of Su. By this time, Di Xin was becoming lazier and more interested in partying than ruling. As a way of pleasing the emperor, the Lord of Su offered him something very special – his daughter, Da Ji. The old emperor fell instantly in love, and spent all his time and money on Da Ji...

... AND I WANT A ZOO OF MY FAVOURITE ANIMALS, AND HUNDREDS OF PAIRS OF SHOES... AND MEAT! IN THE TREES!

YES, MY LOVE. WHATEVER YOU SAY, MY LOVE.

WAIT, WHAT?
TO PRONOUNCE THESE WORD, SAY:
DI XIN = DEE SHIN
DA JI = DAH ZHEE

DA JI

GIRLS JUST WANT TO HAVE FUN! NOW MAKE THE PALACE BIGGER!

THE HISTORY...

As the emperor's favourite consort, Da Ji got everything she wanted – and she wanted a LOT. She made the court play party music all the time. She also got the emperor to build a huge palace, with a wine lake and a forest hung with delicious meats. Da Ji, the emperor and their friends ran around naked, eating the meats and drinking the wine. The people had to give huge taxes to pay for the luxury lifestyle of the emperor and his consort.

Am I what I really seem?

But there are legends about Da Ji too. She had an evil side, and was said to have laughed as she watched people being **EXECUTED**. She is also said to have invented a terrible punishment in which her enemies were tied to a hot metal pole. It was said she would laugh while watching this. Some even said she was not a woman at all, but a silvery fox spirit in human form. After thousands of years, the fox spirit was summoned to **CORRUPT** Di Xin so that his people would get rid of him. Legend says Da Ji was promised she would become **IMMORTAL** if she did this.

THE PLANETS ALIGN

Di Xin and Da Ji were very unpopular. They were cruel, forgot the people, and everyone was becoming poor. It was starting to become clear that the gods were not pleased, and it is said that a series of signs told them their fears were true.

LET'S STOP THIS SILLINESS!

WE GOT RID OF THE LAST GUY WHO WAS THIS BONKERS!

GET RID OF HIM AT ONCE!

IN THE STARS

The Shang believed the stars were living spirits who watched over them, and could punish them if they wanted to. One day, in May 1058 BC, a very unusual thing happened — five planets began to group together in the sky. Could this be a sign from the gods? People started to say the heavens had turned against the emperor.

20

SHANGDI, EMPEROR OF THE GODS

HAVE YOU HEARD THE WORD OF THE BIRD?

Next, a great red bird was said to have landed on the altar at the emperor's temple. The bird is said to have spoken to the people, telling them that the emperor must be overthrown.

Oi! This is not how you're supposed to rule at all! The people are starving and you're supposed to be in charge! You're fired!

Heaven has commanded that the emperor of the Shang must be overthrown! Well? What are you waiting for?

The people could see that the emperor had lost the favour of the gods. Di Xin and Da Ji's time was up...

21

THE BATTLE OF MUYE

Your highness! The Zhou are coming. Your highness? I don't think he can hear me over that awful music.

In the nearby kingdom of the Zhou, times had been good and the Zhou people were getting stronger. Their leader, King Wen, heard of the signs and started to think it might be up to him to get rid of Di Xin and Da Ji.
A messenger heard about this and told Di Xin that the Zhou were coming.

When the messenger arrived, the emperor was dancing with Da Ji. He asked for his army to be sent to meet the Zhou. However, most of the army had been sent away and there was nobody to protect the emperor. Di Xin made a new army of slaves and prisoners, and gathered together all the **PEASANTS**. He had an army now. Sort of...

> WHAT DO YOU MEAN, "COME AND JOIN THE ARMY"? I'VE BEEN SLAVING AWAY ALL DAY WHILE THAT CHUMP FLOATS ABOUT IN HIS STUPID LAKE. WHAT? YOU'RE SAYING I HAVE TO BECAUSE I'M A SLAVE? FINE. BUT I'M NOT HAPPY ABOUT IT.

> WELL, LADS. LOOKS LIKE THE GODS (AND MOST OF DI XIN'S PEOPLE) ARE ON MY SIDE AFTER ALL! ATTACK!

KING WEN

周文王（？—前1046） 明人绘

The two armies met, but then something happened that **Di Xin** didn't expect. Because everyone hated him so much, many of the peasants and slaves threw down their spears and refused to fight. A lot of the soldiers who also hated **Di Xin** did the same thing, and they all joined the side of the Zhou. Those who stayed loyal were all killed. This battle became known as the Battle of Muye. It was named after the place where the battle happened.

23

INTO THE FIRE

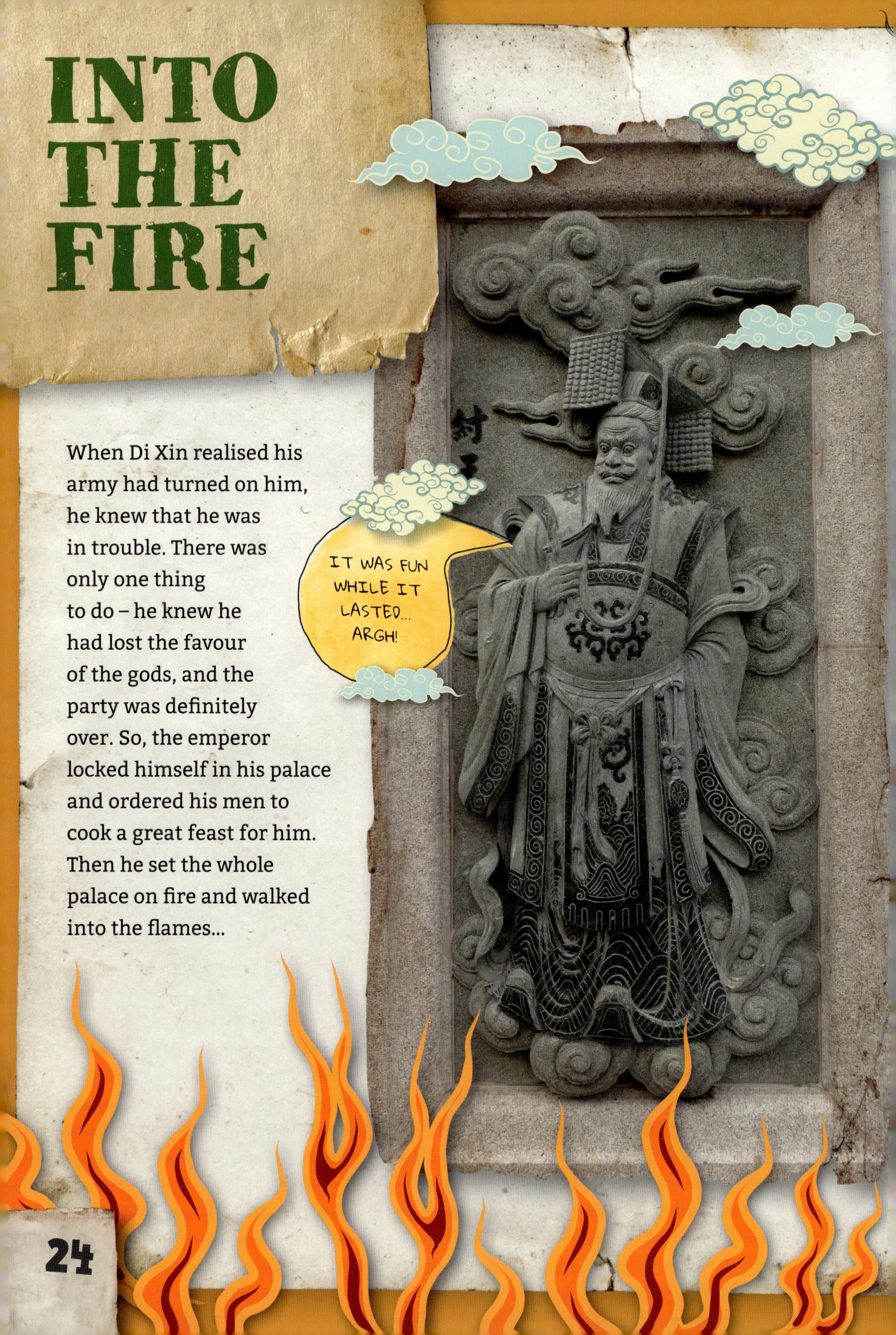

When Di Xin realised his army had turned on him, he knew that he was in trouble. There was only one thing to do – he knew he had lost the favour of the gods, and the party was definitely over. So, the emperor locked himself in his palace and ordered his men to cook a great feast for him. Then he set the whole palace on fire and walked into the flames...

IT WAS FUN WHILE IT LASTED... ARGH!

Historians aren't sure what happened to the wicked Da Ji. Some say that she was executed by the Zhou. Whatever happened, we are sure she didn't survive the battle.

Sigh. Of course they blame it all on me. Di Xin was pretty mean before I came along. I guess the party is really over now... Oh well... byeeeeeeeee!

KING WEN

Looks like I'm in charge now. Better start my own dynasty... just as soon as we put this fire out, of course.

RISE AND FALL

CULTURE, COUNTRY OR CIVILISATION?

It's a pattern we see all the time. Dynasties start off well, having taken over from a corrupt government or a **TYRANT** of a ruler. They set out to do better, to stay true to their people. However, as generation after generation of their children are born to rule, eventually the money and power gets the better of them. The story of the Shang dynasty is a complete circle – from Tang's takeover of the Xia dynasty to the corrupt Di Xin and his consort, Da Ji.

Good. No forests of meat in these plans.

FLICK BACK THROUGH THIS BOOK AND SEE IF YOU CAN SPOT THE SIMILARITIES BETWEEN THE STORY OF JIE AND MO XI AND THAT OF DI XIN AND DA JI.

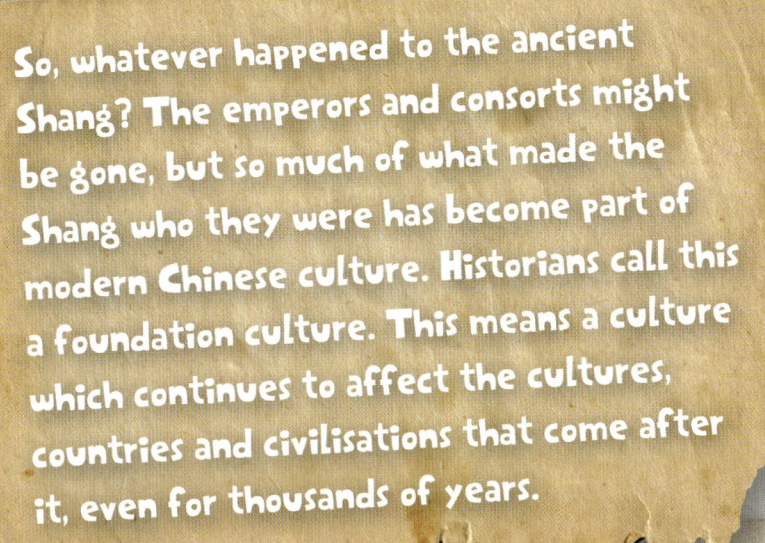

So, whatever happened to the ancient Shang? The emperors and consorts might be gone, but so much of what made the Shang who they were has become part of modern Chinese culture. Historians call this a foundation culture. This means a culture which continues to affect the cultures, countries and civilisations that come after it, even for thousands of years.

The ancient Shang affected language, writing, medicine, metalwork, ideas, beliefs, politics and culture today. If we say that these were the things that made them who they were, can we say they really went anywhere at all?

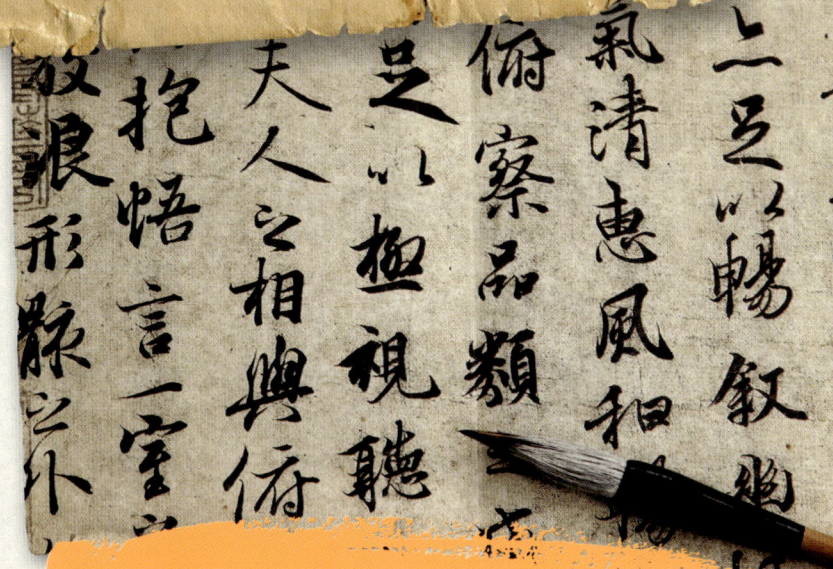

THE PICTOGRAMS, OR PICTURE-WRITING, ON THIS ANCIENT SHANG ORACLE BONE ARE SIMILAR TO THOSE USED TODAY.

HAVE WE BEEN FORGOTTEN, DARLING DI XIN?

OH NO, DEAR DA JI. NOBODY'S GOING TO FORGET US IN A HURRY! WE'RE ABSOLUTELY BONKERS!

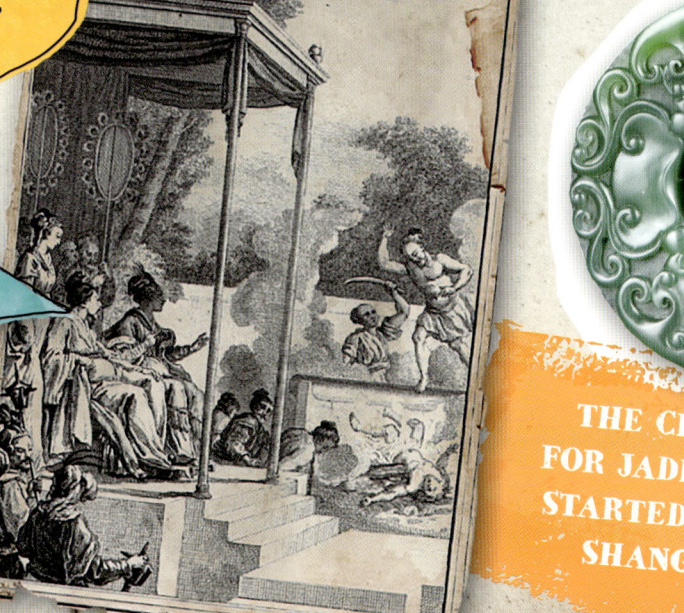

THE CHINESE LOVE FOR JADE MIGHT HAVE STARTED DURING THE SHANG DYNASTY.

27

WHAT REMAINS OF THE ANCIENTS?

China today is a modern place, with bustling cities and a thriving culture all of its own. But if you travel to modern-day China, you can still see signs of how the Shang dynasty changed the country. China might be different now, but the Shang's history is all around us in the present day.

MODERN-DAY BEIJING LOOKS VERY DIFFERENT TO HOW A SHANG VILLAGE WOULD HAVE LOOKED.

WRITING

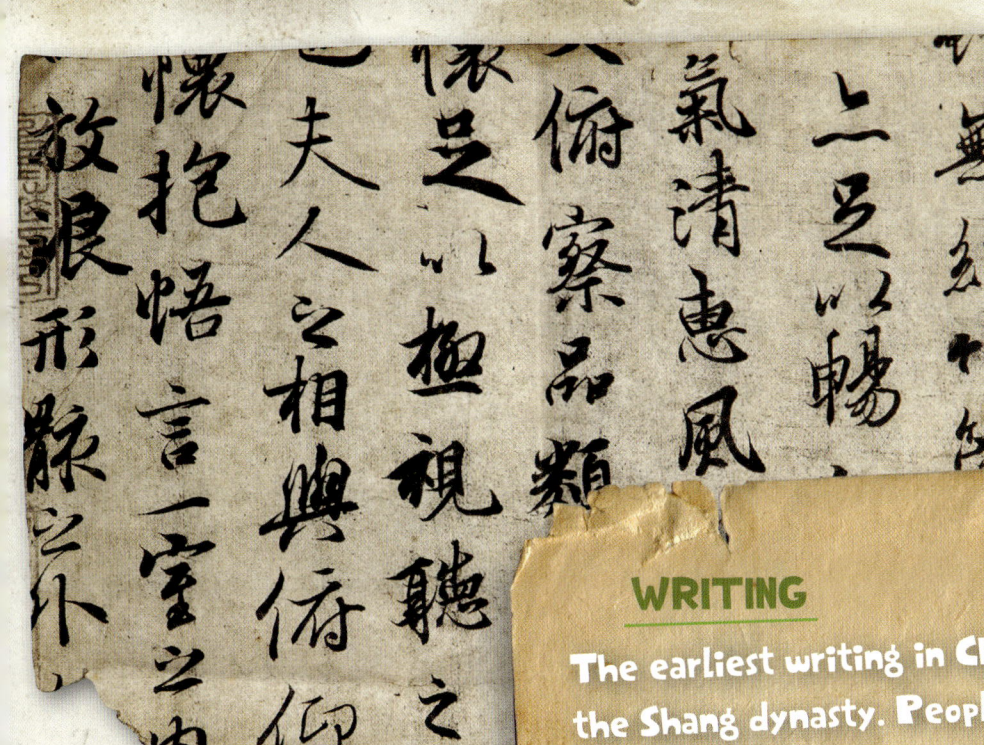

The earliest writing in China comes from the Shang dynasty. People in China don't use letters to spell out different words like people in Western countries do. Instead, each word has its own picture. When historians discovered some ancient oracle bones in a place called Anyang, they were very excited to find they could still read some of the writing! This is because some Chinese writing hasn't changed for thousands of years...

THIS IS THE MODERN CHINESE CHARACTER FOR RAIN. THE CHARACTER HASN'T CHANGED MUCH SINCE ANCIENT TIMES.

SILK

The Shang may not have invented silk, but they definitely found ways of making silk fabric that stayed unchanged for a long, long time. The way they made silk was so valuable that it was kept secret, and anyone caught telling the secret or taking silkworms out of the country was put to death!

GLOSSARY

CAPITAL CITIES
the cities that contain the government

CHANCELLOR
an important member of the government

CIVILISATIONS
certain societies or large groups of people that live in certain areas

CONCUBINE
a woman who lives with a king or emperor and acts like his wife, although she is not his wife

CONSORTS
husbands, wives or close helpers of a king or queen

CORRUPT
to be dishonest and bad in order to become rich and powerful

CULTURE
the way of life and traditions of a group of people

DIVINATION
finding out the future by supernatural means

DROUGHT
a time where there is very little water, which causes death and damage

DYNASTY
a line of rulers who are related to each other

EMPERORS
the rulers of an empire

EMPIRE
a group of countries or states that are owned by one ruler or country

EXECUTED
killed by a ruler or government for breaking their rules

FERTILE
good for growing lots of plants

GONG
something made from metal that makes a loud ringing sound when struck with a stick or hammer

ICONIC
when something is well known and a symbol of a place or time

IMMORTAL
able to live forever

ORACLE BONES
bones used for telling the future

ORACLES
people who give advice or tell the future, often by talking to the gods

PEASANTS
poor farm workers

PROSPERITY
being rich and successful

REIGN
the time that a certain leader rules for

REVOLT
a protest, often violent, to overthrow rulers

SACRIFICE
an object or living thing which is destroyed to please a god or gods

SCRIBES
people who write and copy things out

SOCIAL CLASSES
types of people with different amounts of power

STATE
an area of land in which the people are ruled by one government

TAXES
money that is paid to the people who rule a country or place

TYRANT
a cruel, bad ruler

WINE
a type of drink for adults

INDEX

A
army 15, 23–24

B
Battle of Mingtiao 10
Battle of Muye 22–23
bronze 4, 6, 14

F
fire 13, 24–25
fox spirit 19

J
jade 7, 27
Jie of the Xia 8–11, 26

L
lakes of wine 8, 18
Lord of Su 17

M
Mandate of Heaven 7
Mo Xi 8–9, 26

O
oracle bones 4, 13, 15, 27, 29

P
peasants 23
planets 20

S
Shangdi 7, 21
silk 29
slaves 7, 23
spirits 19–20
stars 12, 20

T
taxes 8, 10, 18

W
writing 4, 6, 13, 27, 29

X
Xia dynasty 8–11, 26

Y
Yellow River 14

Z
Zhou dynasty 7, 22–23, 25

PHOTO CREDITS

All images are courtesy of Shutterstock.com, unless otherwise specified. With thanks to Getty Images, Thinkstock Photo and iStockphoto. Front Cover – ZaZa Studio, Ian Winslow, ActiveLines, Paragorn Dangsombroon. 4&5 – Monkey Business Images, maria efimova, Meiqianbao, Chris Gyford. 6&7 – Artem Avetisyan, Gurdjieff, Andrea Izzotti, Jade Emperor. 8&9 – Sasin Paraksa, lukpedclub, baoyan, National Palace Museum, Taipei. 10&11 – cornfield, Rama, National Palace Museum, Taipei, Szilas, Zerbor, John Lock. 12&13 – Susii, Coca coco. 14&15 – Mo Wu, Yuan Cao, Chris Gyford. 16&17 – PHGCOM, Marzolino, Katsushika Hokusai. 18&19 – ensiferum, Alewiena_design, lynea. 20&21 – DONGSEUN YANG, JEEPNEX, YulyYulia, gyn9037. 22&23 – John Lock, elwynn. 24&25 – aSuruwataRi, Nipatsara Bureepia, Photo Dharma, WarmTail. 26&27 – imtmphoto, Sun Xuejun, Sophy Ru, MOAimage. 28&29 – HelloRF Zcool, Erena.Wilson. Paper – ZaZa Studio, Monica Butnaru, Ints Vikmanis, Anton Watman. Speech Bubbles – Nataleana. Caption banner – Olga_C